MEDITERRANEAN DIET COOKBOOK

50 EASY FLAVORFUL RECIPES FOR LIFELONG HEALTH

EMMA FISHBONE

Table of Contents

Introduction

The Mediterranean diet is a diet inspired by the eating habits of Greece, Italy, Spain, and the countries bordering the Mediterranean Sea. The main aspects of this diet include high consumption of olive oil, legumes, cereals, fruits and vegetables, medium/high consumption of fish, moderate consumption of dairy products (especially cheese and yogurt), moderate consumption of wine and low consumption of meat products. Studies have shown that olive oil plays an important part in reducing all-cause mortality and chronic disease. In fact, the Mediterranean diet, as a whole, is also known to reduce all-cause mortality. There is also evidence that the Mediterranean diet minimizes the risk of heart disease, diabetes and premature death. The Mediterranean diet can aid weight loss in overweight people. The Mediterranean diet is one of three healthy diets recommended in the U.S. Dietary Guidelines, which also include the dash diet or a vegetarian diet. The Mediterranean diet as a nutritional recommendation is different from the cultural practices that UNESCO listed in 2010 under the heading "Mediterranean diet" on the Representative List of the Intangible Cultural Heritage of Humanity: "a set of skills, knowledge, rituals, symbols, and traditions concerning the cultivation, harvesting, fishing, raising, preserving, processing, cooking, and especially sharing and eating of food," not as a set of foods.

Mediterranean Diet

People from Mediterranean countries are known to live longer and healthier lives compared to most Americans. There are many reasons for this, however the main cause is the difference in lifestyles and diets. Not that Mediterranean natives are spared from evil diseases such as cancer or heart failures, but the number of such illnesses is significantly lower.

When you hear about the Mediterranean, the first thing that comes to your mind is the great food, delicious wine, sunshine, lovely islands and people who look utterly content. There is no secret, these people tend to eat lots of fresh fruits and vegetables. Some of the best Mediterranean meals contain nothing but vegetables and olive oil.

So, when your diet is mainly based on eating fruits, vegetables, fish, nuts, and healthy oils, it is no wonder that your body is fit and you are not as prone to diseases such as diabetes and cancer.

The Mediterranean diet is not a new thing. People living around the Mediterranean Sea (Balkans, Italy, Spain, Turkey, etc.) always consumed local produce.

The popularity of this diet rose in the sixties when Mediterranean restaurants found their way to the rest of the world.

The secret lies in the fact that the Mediterranean Diet is focused on whole-grain foods, healthy fats (olive oil, nuts, fish), fruits, vegetables, and small amounts of red meat.

But what most people do not know about this diet is the fact that it encourages people to cook and eat their meals with their families. Naturally, for an even better result, the Mediterranean Diet is twice as effective if coupled with physical activity.

People who live around the Mediterranean are known hedonists; they love good food and good drinks, do not rush their meals, and dedicate their attention to the food they eat. But, besides the good food, they are not lazy and would gladly use their bike or walk from one place to another.

Every meal in this diet is as equally as important, and you are not advised to starve to see visible results in your body.

This diet requires you to start the day with a light breakfast, such as oatmeal. Naturally, a light breakfast will not keep you full for a long time; therefore, the Mediterranean Diet suggests a piece of fruit as a snack between breakfast and lunch.

Lunch usually includes a delicious salad that contains lots of vegetables mixed with cheese or nuts, while dinner is reserved for a more substantial dish (fish, vegetables, cuscus, etc.). Unlike many diets, the Mediterranean Diet will not restrain you from eating starchy foods or foods rich in carbohydrates. On the contrary, this diet does not consider such foods bad.

The main reason for that is because carbs are not bad per se, when mixed with the right amount of healthy fats (fish and other seafood), vegetables and fruits, carbs cannot harm your body.

Carbohydrates are only bad for your health and weight if consumed in excessive amounts, without eating vegetables, fruits and good fats.

In this case, your body will only focus on burning the carbs to create glucose (the essential brain's energy supply), whilst the fats remain stored in layers around your stomach, arms, and legs.

A more straightforward answer would be to say that there is no defined Mediterranean Diet, as one can't expect people in Italy to eat the same meals as people in France or Spain, for example.

The similarity lies in the way these people fill their plates and most importantly, what ingredients they use.

Although it is called a Mediterranean Diet, it is, in fact, an eating pattern. It is not a diet in the literal meaning of the word. For this reason, people love it and tend to find it easier to use in their everyday lives, as unlike other diets it doesn't restrict you from eating or not eating certain foods.

It is up to you to decide what foods are suitable for your body, how many calories you need to lose, what activities are necessary for you to get your body into good shape. This is how you will create your Mediterranean diet menu.

The so-called Mediterranean diet pyramid is the best indicator to help you start and create every meal of your day.

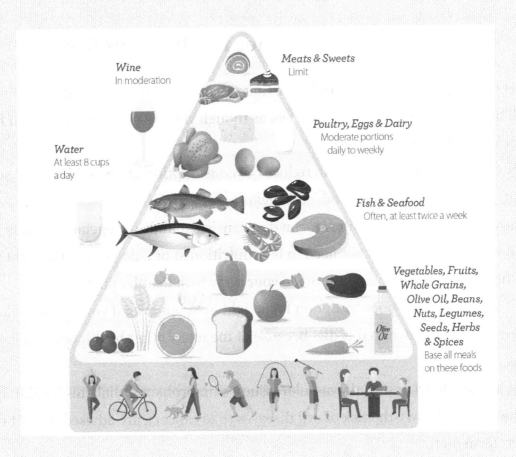

This pyramid puts an emphasis on consuming vegetables, fruits, whole grains, nuts, olive oil, herbs and spices, fish, seafood, beans and legumes at least five times in the week. What is impressive about this diet is the fact that nothing is forbidden; there are priority foods and foods that should be eaten less frequently.

When it comes to alcoholic drinks, this diet is allowing red wine, but only in moderation. One glass of red wine is more than enough for women, and two for men; but wine is not a must. Include it if you feel like drinking it and if your doctor allows it.

The most important thing to remember is to include physical activity several times per week. You can start with something light, such as simple hiking or walking instead of using your car or the bus.

If exercise is not your favorite thing and you do not feel like hiking or walking, you can always try something else like dance classes or even gardening.

Mediterranean Diet Health Benefits

This diet is known as perhaps the only one that provides you with good health long-term. You will never feel hungry, nor will you feel as though you are preventing yourself from eating delicious foods.

The only thing this diet requires is to reduce the consumption of unhealthy foods such as red meat, junk food, processed food, and sugars.

As already mentioned, the Mediterranean diet consists mainly of vegetables, fruits, seeds, fish, and legumes and you do not need to be a nutritionist or a doctor to know that a diet rich in such foods is a sure way to provide your body with healthy nutrients.

This diet is an extremely popular option for weight loss, but even if you are not willing to slim down, you can switch to this diet because of the many other health benefits it provides.

People who have heart and cardiovascular issues, skin problems, diabetes, or simply want to stay healthy and lower the risk of evil diseases (like cancer), are advised to start the Mediterranean diet.

Let's look at the health benefits that this diet brings.

Reduced Risk of Heart Failures

Providing your body with colorful meals that contain large amounts of fruits, vegetables, healthy oils, and less processed food or unhealthy ingredients is a sure way to remain in good health.

New England Journal of Medicine published a study in 2013 that was following more than 7000 people (men and women) in Spain who were suffering type 2 diabetes. They were at high risk for cardiovascular illnesses; the ones that were following the Mediterranean diet (plenty of vegetables, fruits, fish, and olive oil) had about 30% lower risk of heart failures. The researchers did not encourage the participants to exercise (the study wanted to see only the results of the diet).

The study reanalyzed the data in 2018, and they came with similar results.

Consuming large amounts of fish instead of red meat is the key to a healthy heart; the risk for seizures, heart attacks, cholesterol and premature death is reduced.

Prevents Alzheimer's Disease and Memory Decline

The Mediterranean way of eating will help your brain stay in good shape. As we get older, our memory tends to decline, and the brain's activity significantly drops.

The human brain needs food to function properly and when that food we eat is unsuitable, the risk of diseases such as Alzheimer's increases.

Our brains need quality nutrients and oxygen and the best way to provide that is by the eating the right foods.

Food that is not providing our blood with enough oxygen will manifest in poor memory and cognitive functioning.

In 2016 the Journal Frontiers in Nutrition was monitoring the effect of the Mediterranean diet on the cognitive functions. The results showed that this diet does improve brain functioning and slows down memory declining.

Weight Loss and Healthy Weight Maintenance

Switching from a regular (mostly unhealthy) diet to the Mediterranean pattern of eating is a quite common thing. This way of eating is not a new thing, nor was it created by nutritionists.

This diet is part of a regular lifestyle for the people who live around the Mediterranean (Spain, France, Italy, Balkan countries).

The menu consists of foods that are native to the area, mainly fruits, vegetables, seeds, fish, nuts, herbs.

What makes this eating pattern so suitable for weight loss is the fact that it suggests consuming fresh and whole food without additional additives that only add flavor and make you crave more unhealthy foods. The purging effect of fruits, vegetables, nuts, and healthy fats like olive oils cleanses your body from fat and cholesterol and helps in the slimming process.

The body is now provided with healthy nutrients that are easy for digestion. Healthy fats (olive oil, avocado, nuts) provide the brain and the body with enough energy, while the rest of the ingredients are not layered in fats all over the body.

Consuming this calorie-unrestricted Mediterranean eating pattern for five years will keep your weight balanced. The food combination in its suggested amounts (daily, weekly, and monthly) will result in healthy weight loss.

If your goal is to lose a larger amount of weight, you can combine the Mediterranean diet with calorie restriction and physical activity.

Mediterranean Diet Helps in Managing Type 2 Diabetes

People who have type 2 diabetes are advised to follow diets that are not rich in carbohydrates and sugars. The Mediterranean diet might be a good solution for them too. This diet is all about whole grains and healthy carbohydrates, which will not increase the blood sugar levels. Complex whole-grain carbohydrates (quinoa, wheat berries, or buckwheat) are a far better option than refined carbohydrates (white bread, sweets, juices, chocolate, fast food).

Studies show that people aged 50 to 80 years, who were diabetes-free and followed the Mediterranean diet for three to four years, did not develop the disease.

These people used olive oil and nuts, and in general, ate whole food and fish instead of processed food and meats. They had a 52% lower risk for type 2 diabetes.

Mediterranean Diet Reduces the Risk of Some Cancers

Food can be both cure and poison. When your daily menu contains foods rich in unhealthy fats (palm oil, butter), red meat, processed food, sugars, and large amounts of proteins (mostly from red meat) and carbohydrates (unhealthy options such as cookies, white bread, rice, French fries, etc.) – your body will suffer in the long run.

Most cancers are a result of poor eating habits, lack of physical activity, polluted air, and so on.

The Mediterranean diet helps in reducing the risk of cancers like colorectal, gastric, and breast cancer. The high intake of vegetables, fruits, and whole grains play a powerful role in keeping you healthy and in good shape.

Women who follow this diet (and use extra-virgin olive oil) have a 62% lower risk of breast cancer; studies show.

Mediterranean Diet Can Help with Anxiety and Depression

Almost everyone has experienced occasional depression (due to stress, problems in the family, or work).

Depression is a persistent loss of enthusiasm and enjoyment in doing things you once liked doing. Despair, lethargy, disinterest, sleeping problems are just a few of the symptoms of depression.

Anxiety, on the other hand, often manifests with nervousness before significant events, speaking to people, and meeting new people, going out, making mistakes, fear of arguments. Sweaty palms, irritable bowel movement, overthinking, lack of sleep, and intrusive thoughts that you are not good enough or not doing things good enough are just a few of the symptoms.

Psychologists say that diet and mental health are tightly connected. Foods packed in healthy ingredients can seriously improve your general health, including your energy levels and mental state.

If you are avoiding processed foods rich in unhealthy fats, red meat, white bread, and sugars, you will witness significant changes in every area of your life.

Change of lifestyle (new eating habits and physical activity) can improve depression and anxiety symptoms. Good, healthy and quality food impacts moods and increases levels of serotonin. When physical activity is added, depression becomes less severe. Naturally, you need to seek professional help from a therapist, but a change in your diet could only bring positive changes.

This diet also affects the immune system, which is one of the main factors in the risk of depression.

Mediterranean diet prevents inflammations, as well. Most bacteria are fed by sugars and processed food nutrients, so when you change that and provide your body with fresh food, fish, nuts, olive oil, and whole-grain carbohydrates, you are reducing the risk of inflammation.

When your body is at a high risk of inflammation, it is more prone to depression.

According to the studies published in The Journal of Clinical Psychiatry, depressed people have a 46% higher risk of inflammatory diseases in their blood.

The Mediterranean diet is packed with anti-inflammatory foods – olive oil, leafy greens, nuts, salmon, sardines, oranges, strawberries are just some of the foods that fight inflammation.

On the other hand, foods like margarine, red meat, processed meat, deep-fried foods, white bread, soft drinks (soda and tetra pack juices) are not recommended, not only because they are not healthy, but because they are known for their inflammatory properties.

Meal Plan 14 days

Day	Non-Fasting Breakfast Recipes	Non-Fasting Lunch or Dinner Recipes	Non-Fasting Snack Recipes
1	Mediterranean Breakfast Salad	Grilled Steak, Mushroom, and Onion Kebabs	Mediterranean Tomato Salad with Feta and Fresh Herbs
2	Smoked Salmon and Poached Eggs on Toast	Turkey Meatballs	Quinoa Bowl with Yogurt, Dates, And Almonds
3	Honey Almond Ricotta Spread with Peaches	Chicken Marsala	Almond Butter Banana Chocolate Smoothie
4	Mediterranean Eggs Cups	Cauliflower Steaks with Eggplant Relish	Vanilla Apple Compote
5	Low-Carb Baked Eggs with Avocado and Feta	Lemon Caper Chicken	Strawberry Rhubarb Smoothie
6	Mediterranean Eggs White Breakfast Sandwich with Roasted Tomatoes	Herb Roasted Chicken	Apple Dates Mix
7	Greek Yogurt Pancakes	Mediterranean Bowl	Walnut & Date Smoothie

8	Mediterranean Feta and Quinoa Egg Muffins	Tasty Lamb Leg	Lemon Pear Compote
9	Mediterranean Eggs	Kale Sprouts & Lamb	Strawberry Stew
10	Pastry-Less Spanakopita	Pistachio-Crusted Whitefish	Oat and Fruit Parfait
11	Date and Walnut Overnight Oats	Grilled Fish on Lemons	Blueberry Frozen Yogurt
12	Greek Quinoa Breakfast Bowl	Weeknight Sheet Pan Fish Dinner	Deliciously Cold Lychee Sorbet
13	Mediterranean Frittata	Crispy Polenta Fish Sticks	Tostadas
14	Honey-Caramelized Figs with Greek Yogurt	Crispy Homemade Fish Sticks Recipe	Mediterranean Baked Apples

Breakfast Recipes

Mediterranean Breakfast Salad

Preparation Time: 10 Minutes

Cooking Time: 20 Minutes

Servings: 4

Ingredients:

4 whole eggs

2 cups of cherry tomatoes or heirloom tomatoes cut in half or wedges

10 cups of arugula

A 1/2 chopped seedless cucumber

1 large avocado

1 cup cooked or cooled quinoa

1/2 cup of chopped mixed herbs like dill and mint

1 cup of chopped Almonds

1 lemon

extra virgin olive oil

sea salt

freshly ground black pepper

Directions:

In this recipe, the eggs are the first thing that need to be cooked. Start with soft boiling the eggs. To do that, you need to add water to a pan, bring to a boil, reduce heat to simmer and lower the eggs into the water and let them cook for about 6 minutes. After they are boiled, wash the eggs in cold water and set aside. Peel them when they are cool and ready to use.

Combine quinoa, arugula, cucumbers, and tomatoes in a bowl and drizzle with a little olive oil. Season with salt and pepper and toss to season equally.

Once all that is done, serve the salad on four plates and garnish with sliced avocados and the halved eggs. After that, season it with some more salt and pepper.

Finally, top it off with almonds and sprinkle some herbs along with some lemon zest and olive oil.

Nutrition:

calories: 85

protein: 3.4 g

fat: 3.46 g

carbs: 6.71 g

Smoked Salmon and Poached Eggs on Toast

Preparation Time: 10 Minutes

Cooking Time: 4 Minutes

Servings: 4

Ingredients:

2 oz avocado mashed

2 slices of bread, toasted

Pinch of kosher salt and cracked black pepper

1/4 tsp freshly squeezed lemon juice

2 eggs see notes, poached

3.5 oz smoked salmon

1 TBSP. thinly sliced scallions

Splash of Kikkoman soy sauce optional

Microgreens are optional

Directions:

Mash avocado in a small bowl. Add lemon juice and a pinch of salt, mix well and set aside.

Next, poach the eggs and toast your bread

Once the bread is toasted, spread the avocado mix on both slices and add smoked salmon to each slice.

Transfer the poached eggs to the respective toasts.

Add a splash of Kikkoman soy sauce and some cracked pepper and lastly, garnish with scallions and microgreens.

Nutrition:

Calories: 459

Protein: 31 g

Fat: 22 g

Carbs: 33 g

Honey Almond Ricotta Spread with Peaches

Preparation Time: 5 Minutes

Cooking Time: 8 Minutes

Servings: 4

Ingredients:

1/2 cup Fisher Sliced Almonds

1 cup whole milk ricotta

1/4 teaspoon almond extract

zest from an orange, optional

1 teaspoon honey

hearty whole-grain toast

English muffin or bagel

extra Fisher sliced almonds

sliced peaches

extra honey for drizzling

Directions:

Cut peaches into wedges and brush with olive oil. Set aside.

Take a bowl to combine the ingredients for the filling. Set aside.

Next pre-heat grill to medium temperature.

Place peaches cut side down onto a greased grill.

Close cover and grill until the peaches have softened, approximately 6-10 minutes, depending on the size of the peaches.

Place peach halves onto a serving plate.

Place 1 tablespoon of ricotta mixture into the cavity (you are also allowed to use a small scooper).

Sprinkle it slivered almonds, crushed amaretti cookies, and honey.

Decorate with fresh mint leaves.

Nutrition:

Calories: 187

Protein: 7 g

Fat: 9 g

Carbs: 18 g

Mediterranean Eggs Cups

Preparation Time: 10 Minutes

Cooking Time: 20 Minutes

Servings: 8

Ingredients:

1 dough sheet

1 cup spinach, finely chopped

1/2 yellow onion, finely diced

1/2 cup sliced sun-dried tomatoes

4 large basil leaves, finely chopped

Pepper and salt to taste

1/3 cup feta cheese crumbles

8 large eggs

1/4 cup milk (any kind)

Directions:

Pre-heat oven to 375°F.

Roll your dough into a 12x8-inch rectangle and cut in half lengthways.

Cut your dough halves into 4 pieces (quarters), forming 8 (4x3-inch) pieces of dough.

Then press each piece of dough in and around an ungreased muffin cup.

Trim any excess dough to avoid each cooked cup from touching the other. Set aside.

Next, whisk eggs together with salt & pepper in a bowl. Set aside.

Melt the butter in a 12-inch skillet over a medium heat until sizzling; add bell peppers.

Stirring occasionally, 2-3 minutes or until crisply tender.

After that, add spinach leaves; continue cooking until spinach has wilted. Then add egg mixture and prosciutto.

Divide the mixture evenly among prepared muffin cups.

Finally, bake for 14-17 minutes or until the crust has turned golden brown.

Nutrition:

Calories: 240

Protein: 9 g

Fat: 16 g

Carbs: 13 g

Low-Carb Baked Eggs with Avocado and Feta

Preparation Time: 10 Minutes

Cooking Time: 15 Minutes

Servings: 2

Ingredients:

1 avocado

4 eggs

2-3 tbsp. crumbled feta cheese

Nonstick cooking spray

Pepper and salt to taste

Directions:

First, preheat your oven to 400 degrees F.

When your oven has reached the desired temperature place the gratin dishes directly on the baking sheet.

Heat the dishes oven for approximately 10 minutes.

After this process, you need to crack your eggs into individual ramekins.

Wait for avocado and eggs to reach room temperature, for at least 10 minutes.

Next peel the avocado and cut each one into 6-8 wedges.

Remove the dishes from the oven and spray them with the non-stick spray.

Then place the avocado slices in the dishes and tip two eggs into each dish.

Sprinkle with feta, add salt & pepper to taste.

Nutrition:

Calories: 280

Protein: 11 g

Fat: 23 g

Carbs: 10 g

Mediterranean Eggs White Breakfast Sandwich with Roasted Tomatoes

Preparation Time: 15 Minutes

Cooking Time: 10 Minutes

Servings: 2

Ingredients:

Salt and pepper to taste

¼ cup egg whites

1 teaspoon chopped fresh herbs like rosemary, basil, parsley,

1 whole grain seeded ciabatta roll

1 teaspoon butter

1-2 slices Muenster cheese

1 tablespoon pesto

About ½ cup roasted tomatoes

10 ounces grape tomatoes

1 tablespoon extra-virgin olive oil

Black pepper and salt to taste

Directions:

Start by melting the butter over medium heat in a small nonstick skillet.

Then, mix the egg whites with pepper and salt and sprinkle with the fresh herbs.

After that cook eggs for almost 3-4 minutes or until the eggs are cooked, then flip them carefully.

Meanwhile, toast ciabatta bread in the toaster

Place the cooked egg on the bottom half of your Ciabatta, then top with cheese.

Add roasted tomatoes to the top half of Ciabatta.

To roast tomatos, preheat the oven to 400 degrees.

Then, slice the tomatoes in half lengthwise.

Place on the baking sheet and drizzle with olive oil.

Season with pepper and salt and then roast in the oven for about 20 minutes. Skins will appear wrinkled when done.

Nutrition:

Calories: 458

Protein: 21 g

Fat: 24 g

Carbs: 51 g

Greek Yogurt Pancakes

Preparation Time: 10 Minutes

Cooking Time: 5 Minutes

Servings: 2

Ingredients:

1 cup all-purpose flour

1 cup whole-wheat flour

1/4 teaspoon salt

4 teaspoons baking powder

1 Tablespoon sugar

1 1/2 cups unsweetened almond milk

2 teaspoons vanilla extract

2 large eggs

1/2 cup plain 2% Greek yogurt

Fruit, for serving.

Maple syrup, for serving.

Directions:

Pour curds into a bowl and mix well until creamy.

Add egg whites and mix well until combined.

Pour wet mixture into a mixing bowl and slowly add dry ingredients. Stir to combine. The batter should be extremely thick.

Spoon the batter onto the sprayed pan, heated too medium-high.

Lastly, flip the pancakes once when they begin to bubble a bit on the surface. Cook until golden brown on both sides.

Nutrition:

Calories: 166

Protein: 14 g

Fat: 5 g

Carbs: 52g

Mediterranean Feta and Quinoa Egg Muffins

Preparation Time: 15 Minutes

Cooking Time: 15 Minutes

Servings: 12

Ingredients:

2 cups baby spinach finely chopped

1 cup chopped or sliced cherry tomatoes

1/2 cup finely chopped onion

1 tablespoon chopped fresh oregano

1 cup crumbled feta cheese

1/2 cup chopped {pitted} kalamata olives

2 teaspoons high oleic sunflower oil

1 cup cooked quinoa

8 eggs

1/4 teaspoon salt

Directions:

Pre-heat oven to 350 degrees Fahrenheit

Place 12 silicone muffin holders onto a baking sheet, or you can also grease a 12-cup muffin tin with oil and set aside.

Finely slice the vegetables

Heat the skillet to a medium heat.

Add the vegetable oil and onions and sauté for 2 minutes.

Then, add tomatoes and sauté for another minute, then add spinach and sauté until wilted, about 1 minute.

Put the beaten egg into a bowl and add the vegetables, feta cheese, quinoa, as well as salt and stir well until everything is well-combined.

Pour the mixture into greased muffin tins or silicone cups, dividing the mixture equally.

Then, bake in an oven for 30 minutes or so, or until the eggs set nicely and muffins turn a light golden brown in color.

Nutrition:

Calories: 113

Protein: 6 g

Fat: 7 g

Carbs: 5 g

Mediterranean Eggs

Preparation Time: 15 Minutes

Cooking Time: 20 Minutes

Servings: 2

Ingredients:

5 tbsp. of divided olive oil

2 diced medium-sized Spanish onions

2 diced red bell peppers

2 minced cloves garlic

1 teaspoon cumin seeds

4 diced large ripe tomatoes

1 tablespoon of honey

Salt

Freshly ground black pepper

1/3 cup crumbled feta

4 eggs

1 teaspoon zaatar spice

Grilled pita during serving

Directions:

To begin with, add 3 tablespoons of olive oil to a pan and heat over a medium heat. Add and sauté cumin seeds, onions, garlic, and red pepper for a few minutes.

After that, add the diced tomatoes, salt and pepper and cook for about 10 minutes till they come together and form a light sauce.

With that, half the preparation is already done. Next, crack the eggs directly into the sauce and poach them. However, the goal here is to cook the egg whites but your yolks must remain runny. This takes about 8 to 10 minutes.

While plating add some feta and olive oil with zaatar spice to further enhance the flavors. Once done, serve with grilled pita.

Nutrition:

Calories: 304

Protein: 12 g

Fat: 16 g

Carbs: 28 g

Pastry-Less Spanakopita

Preparation Time: 5 Minutes

Cooking Time: 20 Minutes

Servings: 4

Ingredients:

1/8 teaspoons black pepper, add as per taste

1/3 cup of virgin olive oil

4 lightly beaten eggs

7 cups of Lettuce, preferably a spring mix (mesclun)

1/2 cup of crumbled Feta cheese

1/8 teaspoon of Sea salt, add to taste

1 finely chopped medium Yellow onion

Directions:

For this delicious recipe, you need to start by preheating the oven to 180C and grease a flan dish.

Once done, pour extra virgin olive oil into a large saucepan, add onions and cook over a medium heat until onions are translucent. To that, add greens and keep stirring until all the ingredients have wilted.

Once you have cooked and combined the above ingredients, season with salt and pepper and transfer the greens to the prepared dish and sprinkle on some feta cheese.

Pour the eggs over mixture and bake for 20 minutes till cooked through and slightly brown.

Nutrition:

Calories: 325

Protein: 11.2 g

Fat: 27.9 g

Carbs: 7.3 g

Date and Walnut Overnight Oats

Preparation Time: 5 Minutes

Cooking Time: 20 Minutes

Servings: 2

Ingredients:

¼ Cup Greek Yogurt, Plain

1/3 cup of yogurt

2/3 cup of oats

1 cup of milk

2 tsp date syrup or you can also use maple syrup or honey

1 mashed banana

¼ tsp cinnamon

¼ cup walnuts

pinch of salt (approx.1/8 tsp)

Directions:

Firstly, get a mason jar or a small bowl and add all the ingredients.

After that stir and mix all the ingredients well.

Cover it securely and cool it in a refrigerator overnight.

After that, take it out the next morning, add more liquid or cinnamon if required, and serve cold. (This dish can also be heated in a microwave for those of you who prefer a warm dish)

Nutrition:

Calories: 350

Protein: 14 g

Fat: 12 g

Carbs: 49 g

Greek Quinoa Breakfast Bowl

Preparation Time: 10 Minutes

Cooking Time: 20 Minutes

Servings: 2

Ingredients:

2 large eggs

3/4 cup Greek yogurt

2 cups of cooked quinoa

3/4 cup muhammara

3 ounces of baby spinach

4 ounces of marinated kalamata olives

6 ounces of sliced cherry tomatoes

1 halved lemon

hot chili oil

salt & pepper to taste

fresh dill and sesame seeds to garnish

Directions:

Add all ingredients, Greek yogurt, granulated garlic, onion powder, salt, and pepper, and whisk them all together and set aside.

In a separate large saucepan, heat olive oil on medium-high heat and add spinach. You must cook spinach till it is slightly wilted. This takes about 3-4 minutes.

After that, cook the cherry tomatoes in the same skillet for 3-4 minutes or until they have softened.

Stir in the egg mixture and keep stirring for approx. 7 to 9 minutes until eggs have set and scramble.

After the eggs have set, stir in the quinoa and feta, and cook until it is heated all the way through and serve hot with some fresh dill and sesame seeds to garnish.

Nutrition:

Calories: 357

Protein: 23 g

Fat: 20 g

Carbs: 20 g

Mediterranean Frittata

Preparation Time: 8 Minutes

Cooking Time: 6 Minutes

Servings: 4

Ingredients:

Two teaspoons of olive oil

3/4 cup of baby spinach, packed

Two green onions

Four egg whites, large

Six large eggs

1/3 cup of crumbled feta cheese, (1.3 ounces) along with sun-dried tomatoes and basil

Two teaspoons of salt-free Greek seasoning

1/4 teaspoon of salt

6 chopped olives

Directions:

Add the oil to a ten-inch ovenproof skillet and leave on a medium heat.

While the oil is heating, chop the spinach and onions roughly.

Put the eggs, egg whites, Greek seasoning, olives, cheese, as well as salt in a large mixing bowl and mix thoroughly using a whisker.

Add the chopped spinach and onions to the mixing bowl and stir well.

Pour the mixture into the skillet and cook for 2 minutes or more until the edges of the mixture set. Lift the edges of the mixture gently and tilt the pan so that the uncooked parts of the egg spread and cook evenly. Cook for an additional two minutes so that the whole mixture is cooked thoroughly.

Broil for two to three minutes till the center sets.

Your Frittata is now ready. Cut into quarters and Serve Hot.

Nutrition:

Calories: 178

Protein: 16 g

Fat: 12 g

Carbs: 2.2 g

Honey-Caramelized Figs with Greek Yogurt

Preparation Time: 5 Minutes

Cooking Time: 5 Minutes

Servings: 4

Ingredients:

Four fresh figs, halved

2 tbsp of melted butter, 30ml

2 tbsp of brown sugar, 30ml

2 cups of Greek yogurt 500ml

1/4 cup of honey, 60ml

Directions:

Take a non-stick skillet and preheat over a medium flame.

Add the butter to the pan and be sure to remove the eyes from your figs.

Toss in figs and sprinkle with some brown sugar.

Cook the figs on a medium flame for 2-3 minutes until they turn a golden brown.

Turn the figs over and cook for a further 2-3 minutes.

Remove the figs from the pan and leave to cool slightly.

Place a scoop of Greek yogurt on a plate. Set the cooked figs on the yogurt and drizzle with honey.

Nutrition:

Calories: 350

Protein: 6 g

Fat: 19 g

Carbs: 40 g

Main Courses Recipes

Fish Spaghetti

Preparation Time: 25 minutes

Cooking Time: 12 minutes

Servings: 2

Ingredients:

Fish used: Cod

1,100 lbs. of Cod

0,400 lbs. of Spaghetti

0,220 lbs. Cherry tomatoes

½ Garlic clove

½ tbsp Desalted capers

2 tbsp Chopped parsley

4 tbsp Evo

Pinch of salt and pepper

Directions:

Fresh Cod can be recognized by the firmness of the meat and its white color. It is a fish poor in fats, and it is ideal for those following a low-calorie diet. Prepare a green dip by placing the vegetables, oil, garlic, parsley, capers in a blender. Clean the fish: remove its insides and scale it, then wash it well and disentangle it, keeping aside the head and the central spine. Put a large pan on the stove and gently wilt the green dips; add the cherry tomatoes cut into fillets and cook for 5 minutes. Then add 200 ml of hot water and boil the stock for 15 minutes; add the fish head and bone and continue boiling for another 10 minutes Finally, add the fillets, season with salt and pepper and continue cooking for another 15 minutes, till the sauce has reduced. Cook the spaghetti in abundant salted water; drain them al dente and pour them into the previously prepared fish sauce from which the head and the central bone have been removed. Mix all the ingredients together, serve with pieces of cod as a final garnish.

Nutrition :

Calories – 283

Carbs - 80 g,

Protein - 36.6 g,

Fat – 0.3 g

Fish Tagliolini with Lemon Scent

Preparation Time: 25 minutes

Cooking Time: 15 minutes

Servings: 2

Ingredients:

0,400 lbs. of Tagliolini

2 Medium-sized soles

4 Zucchini

2 Untreated lemons

Pinch of salt and pepper

3 tbsp Evo

1 Leek

2 tbsp of Parsley

½ cup of Sparkling white wine

Directions:

Strip and fillet the sole and crumble the meat.

Wash the leek and zucchini and cut into julienne strips.

Grate the zest of the lemons and squeeze the juice into a bowl.

In a non-stick pan, while the pasta water is heating up, put a little oil and sauté the zucchini along with the leek. After a few minutes, add the sole and let it sauté just a little. Then add the approximate of one finger of sparkling white wine.

Once the wine has evaporated, continue cooking and add the lemon juice.

Add salt and pepper to taste

When the water boils, pour in the pasta and drain when it is tender but still firm (this is called 'al dente').

Add the pasta to the sauce, add lemon zest, and toss for a few minutes.

Before serving, add the chopped parsley.

It boasts a clear prevalence of unsaturated fatty acids over saturated ones and is frequently used in the structuring of diets against hypercholesterolemia and hypertriglyceridemia. Here we have chosen an egg pasta which, thanks to the porosity of the surface, better absorbs the sauce, but you can also try the variant with spaghetti or linguine!

Nutrition :

Calories – 283

Carbs - 80 g,

Protein - 36.6 g,

Fat – 1.4 g

Salmon Zucchini Whole Wheat Spaghetti

Preparation Time: 20 minutes

Cooking Time: 12 minutes

Servings: 2

Ingredients:

0,400 lbs. whole wheat spaghetti

2 tbsp of white soy sauce

0,440 lbs. of smoked salmon

1 onion

1 tbsp Evo

0,440 lbs. of zucchini

0,1 lbs. of chives

Directions:

Finely chop both the onion and chives.

Peel and slice the zucchini into strips.

Mince the smoked salmon.

While the spaghetti is boiling in salted water, lightly cook the onion in a large frying pan with oil, then add the zucchini and season with salt and pepper.

Add half of the chives and finally add the fresh salmon.

Drain the spaghetti when al dente, add to the sauce and cook over medium heat. Stir in the soy cream and pepper.

Serve the noodles rolled into a nest and sprinkle with the remaining chives. Finish off with a drizzle of extra virgin olive oil.

Nutrition :

Calories – 252,

Carbs - 180 g,

Protein - 46.6 g,

Fat - 58.2 g

Cuttlefish and Anchovies Spaghetti

Preparation Time: 20 minutes

Cooking Time: 15 minutes

Servings: 2

Ingredients:

0,440 lbs. of spaghetti

1 medium cuttlefish (about 0,220 lbs.)

4 anchovy fillets

2 garlic cloves

1 cup of dry white wine

4 tbsp Evo

Pinch of chili pepper

Pinch of salt

Directions:

Start by boiling water for the pasta.

Take your garlic, crush it and fry it in a pan with oil for a few minutes. It is only a matter of seasoning your oil by taking on the flavor from the garlic, so once you have done that, remove the garlic from the pan.

After that, place the 4 anchovy fillets in a pan and let them melt over a low heat, mix using a fork.

Now the base for the cuttlefish is ready.

Slice your cuttlefish into small pieces, add to the pan and let it cook on a high flame for 5-6 mins, after that fade with some white wine and let it cook for a further 7-8min and add chili pepper.

Drain the spaghetti while still al dente. Add pasta to your pan and finish cooking with all the other ingredients. When the pasta has softened slightly, plate it and serve.

Nutrition :

Calories – 182,

Carbs - 180 g,

Protein - 66.6 g,

Fat - 38.2 g

Lemon Caper Chicken

Preparation Time: 10 minutes

Cooking Time: 15 minutes

Servings: 2

Ingredients:

2 tbsp of Evo

Chicken breasts (2boneless, skinless, cut in half, pound to ¾ an inch thick)

¼ cup of capers

Lemons 2 (wedges)

1 tsp oregano

1 tsp basil

½ tsp black pepper

Directions:

Take a large skillet and place it on your stove and add the olive oil. Turn the heat to medium and allow it to warm up.

As the oil heats up season each side of your chicken breast with oregano, basil and black pepper.

Place your chicken breast into the hot skillet and cook for 5 mins on each side.

Transfer the chicken from the skillet to your dinner plate. Top with capers and serve with lemon wedges.

Nutrition :

Calories – 182,

Carbs - 3.4 g,

Protein - 26.6 g,

Fat - 8.2 g

Anchovies in Green Sauce

Preparation Time: 30 minutes

Marinating Time: 120 minutes

Servings: 6 (leftover anchovies could be stored in a jar)

Ingredients:

0.440 lbs. of anchovies

1 bunch of parsley

1 garlic clove

1 hot chili pepper (optional)

1 cup of Evo

1 tbsp of vinegar

Fine breadcrumbs

Directions:

Divide the anchovies into fillets, taking care to remove all the bones, then rinse them quickly under running water and pat them dry.

Trim parsley, using only the leaves.

Open the garlic clove and remove the "heart" (i.e. the central bud, which leaves the most persistent smell).

Finely chop the parsley and garlic, add extra-virgin olive oil, the breadcrumbs soaked in vinegar and mix everything together until you have a creamy consistency.

Add the chili pepper (left whole).

Finally, place the anchovies in a container or deep dish and pour over green sauce, making sure anchovies are completely covered.

Nutrition :

Calories – 200,

Carbs - 3.4 g,

Protein - 96.6 g,

Fat - 8.2 g

Anchovies Bruschetta

Preparation Time: 15 minutes

Cooking Time: - minutes

Servings: 2

Ingredients:

8 salted anchovies

4 rip and firm tomatoes

4 Slice of bread

2 tbsp Evo

½ garlic clove

Dried or fresh oregano or fresh Basil (optional)

Directions:

First clean the salted anchovies by removing the bones, fillet them, desalinate them under running water, and then gently pat dry with kitchen paper.

Dress them with oil and thinly sliced or minced garlic.

Wash and dry the tomatoes and cut them into slices, removing the seeds.

Toast the bread. Place the tomato slices on the bread, then the anchovy fillets with a little of their oil and garlic on top. Complete with oregano or basil.

Serve bruschetta right away.

Nutrition:

Calories: 410,

Protein: 36 g,

Carbs: 80 g,

Fat: 20 g

Grilled Steak, Mushroom, and Onion Kebabs

Preparation Time: 10 minutes

Cooking Time: 10 minutes

Servings: 2

Ingredients:

1 lb. of Boneless top sirloin steak,

8 oz white button mushrooms,

1 medium red onion,

4 peeled garlic cloves,

2 Rosemary sprigs,

2 tbsp of Evo

¼ tsp Black pepper

2 tbsp red wine vinegar

¼ tsp sea salt

Directions:

Soak 12 (10-inch) wooden skewers in water. Spray the cold grill with nonstick cooking spray and heat the grill to medium-high.

Cut a piece of aluminum foil into a 10-inch square. Place the garlic and rosemary sprigs in the center, drizzle with 1 tablespoon of oil, and wrap tightly to form a foil packet.

Place on grill and seal the grill cover.

Cut the steak into 1-inch cubes. Thread the beef onto the wet skewers, alternating with whole mushrooms and onion wedges. Spray the kebabs thoroughly with nonstick cooking spray, and sprinkle with pepper.

Cook the kebabs on the covered grill for 5 minutes.

Flip and grill for 5 more minutes while covered.

Unwrap foil packets with garlic and rosemary sprigs and place them into a small bowl.

Carefully strip the rosemary sprigs of their leaves into the bowl and pour in any accumulated juices and oil from the foil packet.

Mix in the remaining 1 tablespoon of oil and the vinegar and salt.

Mash the garlic with a fork and mix all ingredients in the bowl together. Pour over the finished steak kebabs and serve.

Nutrition:

Calories: 410,

Protein: 36 g,

Carbs: 12 g,

Fat: 14 g

Turkey Meatballs

Preparation Time: 10 minutes

Cooking Time: 25 minutes

Servings: 2

Ingredients:

¼ of diced yellow onion,

14 oz of diced artichoke hearts

1 lb. ground turkey

1 tsp dried parsley

1 tsp Oil

4 tbsp chopped basil

Pinch of salt

Directions:

Grease baking sheet and preheat the oven to 350° F.

Place a nonstick medium saucepan on a medium heat, sauté artichoke hearts and diced onions for 5 minutes or until onions are soft.

Meanwhile, in a large bowl, mix parsley, basil and ground turkey with with hands. Season to taste.

Once onion mixture has cooled, add to the bowl and mix thoroughly.

With an ice cream scoop, scoop ground turkey and form balls.

Place on a prepared cooking sheet, pop in the oven and bake until cooked around 15-20 minutes.

Remove from pan, serve and enjoy

Nutrition :

Calories : 283,

Protein : 12 g,

Carbohydrates : 30 g,

Fat: 12 g

Chicken Marsala

Preparation Time: 10 minutes

Cooking Time: 45 minutes

Servings: 2

Ingredients:

2 tablespoons olive oil

4 skinless, boneless chicken breast cutlets

¾ tablespoons black pepper, divided

½ teaspoon kosher salt, divided

8 oz. mushrooms, sliced

4 thyme sprigs

0.2 quarts unsalted chicken stock

0.1 quarts Marsala wine

2 tablespoons olive oil

1 tablespoon fresh thyme, chopped

Directions:

Heat oil in a pan and fry chicken for 4-5 minutes on each side. Remove chicken from the pan and set aside.

In the same pan add thyme, mushrooms, salt, and pepper; stir fry for 1-2 minutes.

Add Marsala wine, chicken broth and cooked chicken. Leave to simmer for 10-12 minutes on a low heat.

Add to a serving dish.

Enjoy.

Nutrition:

Calories – 206,

Fat –17 g,

Carbs – 3 g,

Protein – 8 g

Marinated Swordfish with Lemon and Ginger

Preparation Time: 10 minutes + 3 hours marinating

Cooking Time: - minutes

Servings: 2

Ingredients:

0,500 lbs. swordfish fillet

5 fresh basil leaves

3 lemons

3 tbsp of Evo

1 fresh ginger

Pinch of white pepper

Pinch of salt

Directions:

Squeeze the juice of 4-5 lemons into a small bowl, place the swordfish slices in an ovenproof dish and pour the lemon juice over them, until they are completely covered. Let them marinate in the refrigerator for 2-3 hours.

Remove the dish from the refrigerator and drain the lemon juice from the swordfish slices, dabbing them with kitchen paper.

Grate the peeled ginger root, place the grated pulp in a square of gauze and squeeze hard until you end up with approx. half a tablespoon of ginger juice. Pour it into a bowl and emulsify it with the olive oil, a pinch of salt and a generous amount of ground white pepper.

Place the fish slices on individual plates, drizzle with the ginger-flavored emulsion and sprinkle with 5-6 leaves of fresh basil cut into thin strips.

Before serving, garnish the plates with 2 whole fresh basil leaves and lemon slices.

Nutrition:

Calories – 106,

Fat –37 g,

Protein – 48

Citrus Fruits Marinated Swordfish

Preparation Time: 10 minutes + 3 hours marinating

Cooking Time: - minutes

Servings: 2

Ingredients

0,500 lbs. of swordfish fillet

½ lemon

½ orange

½ garlic clove

2 tbsp of Evo

1 bunch of parsley

Pinch of salt and pepper

Directions:

Squeeze the juice from the lemon and orange and keep the grated rinds for later.

Pour the two juices and the zests into a large bowl.

Finely chop the garlic and incorporate it into the bowl, add the olive oil, salt, and pepper.

Finely chop the fresh parsley and add it to the bowl, mixing well.

Take the slices of swordfish, add them to the sauce and leave them to marinade for 1-2 hours in the fridge.

Take the fish out of the fridge and place swordfish in a serving dish with the marinade.

Serve at the table decorating the plate with slices of citrus fruit.

Nutrition:

Calories – 106,

Fat –37 g,

Protein – 48

Cauliflower Steaks with Eggplant Relish

Preparation Time: 5 minutes

Cooking Time: 25 minutes

Servings: 2

Ingredients:

Small heads cauliflower 2 (about 3 pounds)

¼ tsp kosher or sea salt

¼ tsp smoked paprika.

2 tbsp of Evo

Directions:

Place a large, rimmed baking dish in the oven. Preheat the oven to 400°F.

Stand one head of cauliflower on a cutting board, stem-end down. With a long chef's knife, slice down through the very center of the head, including the stem.

Starting at the cut edge, measure about 1 inch and cut one thick slice from each cauliflower half, including as much of the stem as possible, to make two cauliflower "steaks."

Reserve the remaining cauliflower for another use. Repeat with the second cauliflower head.

Dry each steak well with a clean towel. Sprinkle with salt and smoked paprika evenly over both sides of each cauliflower steak.

In a large skillet over medium-high heat, heat 2 tablespoons of oil. When the oil is hot, add two cauliflower steaks to the pan and cook for about 3 minutes, until golden and crispy. Flip and cook for 2 more minutes.

Transfer the steaks to a plate. Use a pair of tongs to hold a paper towel and wipe out the pan to remove most of the hot oil (which will contain a few burnt bits of cauliflower).

Repeat the cooking process with the remaining 2 tablespoons of oil and the remaining two steaks.

Using oven mitts, carefully remove the baking sheet from the oven and place the cauliflower steaks on the baking sheet.

Roast in the oven for 12 to 15 minutes, until the cauliflower steaks are just fork tender; they should still be somewhat firm. Serve the steaks with the Eggplant Relish Spread, baba ghanoush, or the homemade ketchup.

Nutrition:

Calories – 206,

Fat –17 g,

Carbs – 3 g,

Protein – 8 g

Herb Roasted Chicken

Preparation Time: 20 minutes

Cooking Time: 45 minutes

Servings: 2

Ingredients:

1 tablespoon virgin olive oil

1 whole chicken

2 rosemary sprigs

3 garlic cloves (peeled)

1 lemon (cut in half)

1 teaspoon sea salt

1 teaspoon black pepper

Directions:

Turn your oven to 450 degrees F.

Take your whole chicken and pat it dry using paper towels. Then rub in the olive oil.

Remove the leaves from one of the springs of rosemary and scatter them over the chicken. Sprinkle chicken with sea salt and black pepper. Place the other whole sprig of rosemary into the cavity of the chicken along with garlic cloves and lemon halves.

Place the chicken onto a roasting pan and then place it into the oven. Allow the chicken to bake for 1 hour, then check that the internal temperature has reached at least 165 degrees F. If the chicken begins to brown too much, cover it with foil and return it to the oven to finish cooking.

When the chicken has cooked to the appropriate temperature remove it from the oven. Let it rest for at least 20 minutes before carving.

Serve with a large side of roasted or steamed vegetables or your favorite salad.

Nutrition :

Calories – 309,

Carbs - 1.5 g,

Protein - 27.2 g,

Fat - 21.3 g

Tasty Lamb Leg

Preparation Time: 10 minutes

Cooking Time: 20 minutes

Servings: 2

Ingredients:

2 lbs. leg of lamb, boneless and cut into chunks

1 tbsp. olive oil

1 tbsp. garlic, sliced

1 cup red wine

1 cup onion, chopped

2 carrots, chopped

1 tsp. rosemary, chopped

2 tsp. thyme, chopped

1 tsp. oregano, chopped

1/2 cup beef stock

2 tbsp. tomato paste

Pepper

Salt

Directions:

Add oil to the inner pot of instant pot and set the pot on sauté mode.

Add meat and sauté until browned.

Add remaining ingredients and stir well.

Seal pot with lid and cook on high for 15 minutes.

Once done, allow to release pressure naturally. Remove lid.

Stir well and serve.

Nutrition:

Calories 540,

Fat 20.4 g,

Carbohydrates 10.3 g,

Sugar 4.2 g,

Protein 65.2 g,

Cholesterol 204 mg

Kale Sprouts & Lamb

Preparation Time: 10 minutes

Cooking Time: 30 minutes

Servings: 2

Ingredients:

2 lbs. lamb, cut into chunks

1 tbsp. parsley, chopped

2 tbsp. olive oil

1 cup kale, chopped

1 cup Brussels sprouts, halved

1 cup beef stock

Pepper

Salt

Directions:

Add all ingredients to the inner pot of instant pot and stir well.

Seal pot with lid and cook on high for 30 minutes.

Once done, allow to release pressure naturally. Remove lid.

Serve and enjoy.

Nutrition:

Calories 504,

Fat 23.8 g,

Carbohydrates 3.9 g,

Sugar 0.5 g,

Protein 65.7 g,

Cholesterol 204 mg

Pistachio-Crusted Whitefish

Preparation Time: 10 minutes

Cooking Time: 20 minutes

Servings: 2

Ingredients:

¼ cup shelled pistachios

1 tablespoon fresh parsley

1 tablespoon grated Parmesan cheese

1 tablespoon panko breadcrumbs

2 tablespoons olive oil

¼ teaspoon salt

10 ounces skinless whitefish (1 large piece or 2 smaller ones)

Directions:

Preheat the oven to 350°F and set the rack to the middle position. Line a sheet pan with foil or parchment paper.

Combine all the ingredients except the fish in a mini food processor, and pulse until the nuts are finely ground.

Alternatively, you can mince the nuts with a chef's knife and combine the ingredients by hand in a small bowl.

Place the fish on the sheet pan. Spread the nut mixture evenly over the fish and pat it down lightly.

Bake the fish for 20 to 30 minutes, depending on the thickness, until it flakes easily with a fork.

Keep in mind that a thicker cut of fish takes a bit longer to bake. You will know it's done when it turns opaque, flakes apart easily with a fork, or reaches an internal temperature of 145°F.

Nutrition :

Calories – 185,

Carbs - 23.8 g,

Protein - 10.1 g,

Fat - 5.2 g

Grilled Fish on Lemons

Preparation Time: 10 minutes

Cooking Time: 10 minutes

Servings: 2

Ingredients:

4 (4-ounce) fish fillets, such as tilapia, salmon, catfish, cod, or your favorite fish

Nonstick cooking spray

3 to 4 medium lemons

1 tablespoon extra-virgin olive oil

¼ teaspoon freshly ground black pepper

¼ teaspoon kosher or sea salt

Directions:

Using paper towels pat the fillets dry and let stand at room temperature for 10 minutes. Meanwhile, coat the cold cooking grate of the grill with nonstick cooking spray, and preheat the grill to 400°F, or medium-high heat. Or preheat a grill pan over medium-high heat on the stove top.

Cut one lemon in half and set half aside. Slice the remaining half of that lemon and the remaining lemons into ¼-inch-thick slices. (You should have about 12 to 16 lemon slices.)

In a small bowl, squeeze 1 tablespoon of juice out of the reserved lemon half.

Add the oil to the bowl with the lemon juice and mix well.

Brush both sides of the fish with the oil mixture, and sprinkle evenly with pepper and salt.

Carefully place the lemon slices on the grill (or the grill pan), arranging 3 to 4 slices together in the shape of a fish fillet, and repeat with the remaining slices.

Place the fish fillets directly on top of the lemon slices, and grill with the lid closed. (If you are grilling on the stove top, cover with a large pot lid or aluminum foil.)

Turn the fish halfway through the cooking time only if the fillets are more than half an inch thick.

The fish is done and ready to serve when it just begins to separate into flakes (chunks) when pressed gently with a fork.

Nutrition :

Calories – 185,

Carbs - 23.8 g,

Protein - 10.1 g,

Fat - 5.2 g

Weeknight Sheet Pan Fish Dinner

Preparation Time: 10 minutes

Cooking Time: 10 minutes

Servings: 2

Ingredients:

Nonstick cooking spray

2 tablespoons extra-virgin olive oil

1 tablespoon balsamic vinegar

4 (4-ounce) fish fillets, such as cod or tilapia (½ inch thick)

2½ cups green beans (about 12 ounces)

1-pint cherry or grape tomatoes (about 2 cups)

Directions:

Preheat the oven to 400°F. Coat two large, rimmed baking sheets with nonstick cooking spray.

In a small bowl, whisk together the oil and vinegar. Set aside. Place two pieces of fish on each baking sheet.

In a large bowl, combine the beans and tomatoes. Pour in the oil and vinegar and toss gently to coat.

Pour half of the green bean mixture over the fish on one baking sheet, and the remaining half over the fish on the other.

Turn the fish over and rub it in the oil mixture to coat. Spread the vegetables evenly on the baking sheets so hot air can circulate around them.

Bake for 5 to 8 minutes, until the fish is just opaque and not translucent. The fish is done and ready to serve when it just begins to separate into flakes (chunks) when pressed gently with a fork.

Nutrition :

Calories – 185,

Carbs - 23.8 g,

Protein - 10.1 g,

Fat - 5.2 g

Crispy Polenta Fish Sticks

Preparation Time: 15 minutes

Cooking Time: 10 minutes

Servings: 2

Ingredients:

2 large eggs, lightly beaten 1 tablespoon 2% milk.

1-pound skinned fish fillets (cod, tilapia, or other white fish) about ½ inch thick, sliced into 20 (1-inch-wide) strips

½ cup yellow cornmeal

½ cup whole-wheat panko breadcrumbs or whole-wheat breadcrumbs

¼ teaspoon smoked paprika

¼ teaspoon kosher or sea salt

¼ teaspoon freshly ground black pepper

Nonstick cooking spray

Directions:

Place a large, rimmed baking sheet in the oven. Preheat the oven to 400°F with the pan inside. In a large bowl, mix the eggs and milk.

Using a fork, add the fish strips to the egg mixture and stir gently to coat.

Put the cornmeal, breadcrumbs, smoked paprika, salt, and pepper in a quart-size zip-top plastic bag.

Using a fork or tongs, transfer the fish to the bag, letting the excess egg wash drip off into the bowl before transferring. Seal the bag and shake gently to coat each fish stick completely.

With oven mitts, carefully remove the hot baking sheet from the oven and spray it with nonstick cooking spray.

Using a fork or tongs, remove the fish sticks from the bag and place them on the hot baking sheet, with space between them so the hot air can circulate and crisp them up.

Bake for 5 to 8 minutes, until gentle pressure with a fork causes the fish to flake and serve.

Nutrition :

Calories – 185,

Carbs - 23.8 g,

Protein - 10.1 g,

Fat - 5.2 g

Crispy Homemade Fish Sticks Recipe

Preparation Time: 10 minutes

Cooking Time: 15 minutes

Servings: 2

Ingredients:

½ cup of flour

1 beaten egg

1 cup of flour

½ cup of parmesan cheese

½ cup of breadcrumbs.

Zest of 1 lemon juice

Parsley

Salt

1 teaspoon of black pepper

1 tablespoon of sweet paprika

1 teaspoon of oregano

1 ½ lb. of salmon

Extra virgin olive oil

Directions:

Preheat your oven to about 450 degrees F. Get a bowl, dry your salmon, and season its two sides with the salt.

Then chop into small sizes of 1½ inch length each. Get a bowl and mix black pepper with oregano.

Add paprika to the mixture and blend it. Then spice the fish stick with the mixture you have just made. Get another dish and pour your flours.

You will need a different bowl again to pour your egg wash into. Pick yet the fourth dish, mix your breadcrumb with your parmesan and add lemon zest to the mixture.

Return to the fish sticks and dip each fish into flour such that both sides are coated with flour. As you dip each fish into flour, take it out and dip it into egg wash and lastly, dip it in the breadcrumb mixture.

Do this for all fish sticks and arrange on a baking sheet. Ensure you oil the baking sheet before arranging the stick thereon and drizzle the top of the fish sticks with extra virgin olive oil.

Caution: allow excess flours to fall off a fish before dipping it into other ingredients.

Also ensure that you do not let the coating peel while you add extra virgin olive oil on top of the fishes.

Fix the baking sheet in the middle of the oven and allow it to cook for 13 min. By then, the fishes should be golden brown, and you can collect them from the oven, and you can serve immediately.

Top it with your lemon zest, parsley, and fresh lemon juice.

Nutrition:

119 Cal,

3.4g of fat,

293.1mg of sodium,

9.3g of carbs,

13.5g of protein.

Snack Recipes

Mediterranean Tomato Salad with Feta and Fresh Herbs

Preparation Time: 10 minutes

Cooking Time: 15 minutes

Servings: 2

Ingredients:

5 diced tomatoes

2 oz of crumbled feta cheese

½ cup of chopped fresh dill

½ cup of diced onion,

6 chopped mint leaves,

½ tsp of paprika

3 tbsp of olive oil,

2 tbsp of minced garlic

2 tsp of lemon juice

2 tsp of white wine vinegar

Pinch of salt and black pepper

Directions:

Combine the onions, tomatoes, herbs, and the garlic in a bowl, then season with your spices (salt, black pepper, paprika).

To create the dressing, in a separate bowl first mix the olive oil, vinegar, and lemon juice. Top with feta cheese

Nutrition:

Calories : 125,

Protein : 2 g,

Carbohydrates : 8 g,

Fat: 9g

Quinoa Bowl with Yogurt, Dates, And Almonds

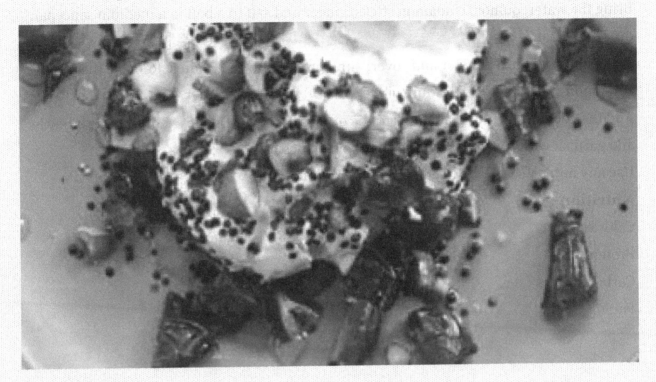

Preparation Time: 10 minutes

Cooking Time: 15 minutes

Servings: 2

Ingredients:

1½ cups water

1 cup quinoa

2 cinnamon sticks

1-inch knob of ginger, peeled

¼ teaspoon kosher salt

1 cup plain Greek yogurt

½ cup dates, pitted and chopped

½ cup almonds (raw or roasted), chopped

2 teaspoons honey (optional)

Directions:

Bring the water, quinoa, cinnamon sticks, ginger and salt to a boil in a medium saucepan over high heat.

Reduce the heat to a simmer and cover; simmer for 10 to 12 minutes. Remove the cinnamon sticks and ginger. Fluff with a fork.

Add the yogurt, dates, and almonds to the quinoa and mix. Divide evenly among 4 bowls and garnish with ½ teaspoon honey per bowl, if desired.

Use any nuts or seeds you like in place of the almonds.

Nutrition :

Calories : 125,

Protein : 2 g,

Carbohydrates : 8 g,

Fat: 9g

Almond Butter Banana Chocolate Smoothie

Preparation Time: 5 minutes

Cooking Time: 30 minutes

Servings: 2

Ingredients:

¾ cup almond milk

½ medium banana, preferably frozen

¼ cup frozen blueberries

1 tablespoon almond butter

1 tablespoon unsweetened cocoa powder

1 tablespoon chia seeds

Directions:

In a blender or Vitamix, add all the ingredients. Blend to combine.

Peanut butter, sunflower seed butter, and other nut butters are good choices to replace the almond butter.

Nutrition :

Calories : 125,

Protein : 2 g,

Carbohydrates : 8 g,

Fat: 9g

Strawberry Rhubarb Smoothie

Preparation Time: 8 minutes

Cooking Time: 0 minutes

Servings: 2

Ingredients:

1 Cup Strawberries, Fresh & Sliced

1 Rhubarb Stalk, Chopped

2 Tablespoons Honey, Raw

3 Ice Cubes

1/8 Teaspoon Ground Cinnamon

½ Cup Greek Yogurt, Plain

Directions:

Start by getting out a small saucepan and filling it with water. Place it over high heat and bring to a boil and add in your rhubarb.

Boil for three minutes before draining and transferring it to a blender.

In your blender add in your yogurt, honey, cinnamon, and strawberries. Blend until smooth, and then add your ice.

Blend until there are no lumps and it is thick. Enjoy cold.

Nutrition:

Calories: 295,

Protein: 6 g,

Fat: 8 g,

Carbs: 56 g

Walnut & Date Smoothie

Preparation Time: 10 minutes

Cooking Time: 0 minutes

Servings: 2

Ingredients:

4 pitted dates

½ Cup Milk

2 Cups Greek Yogurt, Plain

1/2 Cup Walnuts

½ Teaspoon Cinnamon, Ground

½ Teaspoon Vanilla Extract, Pure

2-3 Ice Cubes

Directions:

Blend everything together until smooth, and then serve chilled.

Nutrition:

Calories: 385,

Protein: 21 g,

Fat: 17 g,

Carbs: 35 g

Vanilla Apple Compote

Preparation Time: 10 minutes

Cooking Time: 15 minutes

Servings: 2

Ingredients:

3 cups apples, cored and cubed

1 tsp. vanilla

3/4 cup coconut sugar

1 cup of water

2 tbsp. fresh lime juice

Directions:

Add all ingredients to the inner pot of instant pot and stir well.

Seal pot with lid and cook on high for 15 minutes.

Once done, allow to release pressure naturally for 10 minutes then release remaining pressure using quick release. Remove lid.

Stir and serve.

Nutrition:

Calories 76

Fat 0.2 g

Carbohydrates 19.1 g

Sugar 11.9 g

Protein 0.5 g

Cholesterol 0 mg

Apple Dates Mix

Preparation Time: 10 minutes

Cooking Time: 15 minutes

Servings: 2

Ingredients:

4 apples, cored and cut into chunks

1 tsp. vanilla

1 tsp. cinnamon

1/2 cup dates, pitted

1 1/2 cups apple juice

Directions:

Add all ingredients to the inner pot of instant pot and stir well.

Seal pot with lid and cook on high for 15 minutes.

Once done, allow to release pressure naturally for 10 minutes then release remaining pressure using quick release. Remove lid.

Stir and serve.

Nutrition:

Calories 226

Fat 0.6 g

Carbohydrates 58.6 g

Sugar 46.4 g

Protein 1.3 g

Cholesterol 0 mg

Lemon Pear Compote

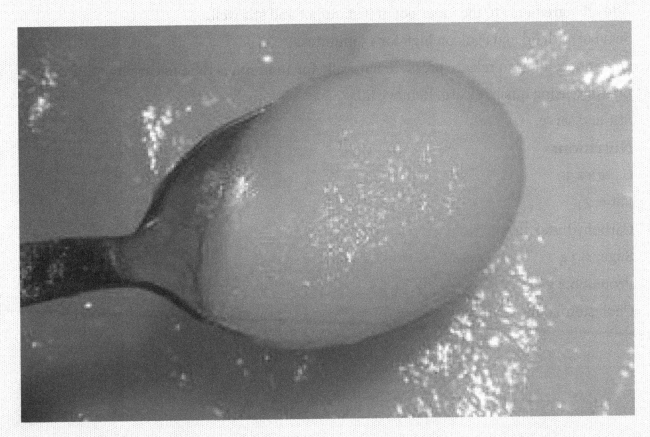

Preparation Time: 10 minutes

Cooking Time: 15 minutes

Servings: 2

Ingredients:

3 cups pears, cored and cut into chunks

1 tsp. vanilla

1 tsp. liquid stevia

1 tbsp. lemon zest, grated

2 tbsp. lemon juice

Directions:

Add all ingredients to the inner pot of instant pot and stir well.

Seal pot with lid and cook on high for 15 minutes.

Once done, allow to release pressure naturally for 10 minutes then release remaining pressure using quick release. Remove lid.

Stir and serve.

Nutrition:

Calories 50

Fat 0.2 g

Carbohydrates 12.7 g

Sugar 8.1 g

Protein 0.4 g

Cholesterol 0 mg

Strawberry Stew

Preparation Time: 10 minutes

Cooking Time: 15 minutes

Servings: 2

Ingredients:

12 oz. fresh strawberries, sliced

1 tsp. vanilla

1 1/2 cups water

1 tsp. liquid stevia

2 tbsp. lime juice

Directions:

Add all ingredients into the inner pot of instant pot and stir well.

Seal pot with lid and cook on high for 15 minutes.

Once done, allow to release pressure naturally for 10 minutes then release remaining pressure using quick release. Remove lid.

Stir and serve.

Nutrition:

Calories 36

Fat 0.3 g

Carbohydrates 8.5 g

Sugar 4.7 g

Protein 0.7 g

Cholesterol 0 mg

Oat and Fruit Parfait

Preparation Time: 10 minutes

Cooking Time: 10 minutes

Servings: 2

Ingredients:

1/2 cup whole-grain rolled or quick cooking oats (not instant)

1/2 cup walnut pieces

1 teaspoon honey

1 cup sliced fresh strawberries

11/2 cups (12 ounces) vanilla low-fat Greek yogurt

Fresh mint leaves for garnish

Directions:

Preheat the oven to 300°F.

Spread the oats and walnuts in a single layer on a baking sheet.

Toast the oats and nuts just until you begin to smell the nuts, 10 to 12 minutes. Remove the pan from the oven and set aside.

In a small microwave-safe bowl, heat the honey just until warm, about 30 seconds. Add the strawberries and stir to coat.

Place 1 tablespoon of the strawberries in the bottom of each of 2 dessert dishes or 8-ounce glasses.

Add a portion of yogurt and then a portion of oats and repeat the layers until the containers are full, ending with the berries. Serve immediately or chill until ready to eat.

Nutrition:

Calories: 385,

Protein: 21 g,

Fat: 17 g,

Carbs: 35 g

Blueberry Frozen Yogurt

Preparation Time: 10 minutes

Cooking Time: 30 minutes

Servings: 2

Ingredients:

1-pint blueberries, fresh

2/3 cup honey

1 small lemon, juiced and zested

2 cups yogurt, chilled

Directions:

In a saucepan, combine the blueberries, honey, lemon juice, and zest.

Heat over medium heat and allow to simmer for 15 minutes while stirring constantly.

Once the liquid has reduced, transfer the fruits in a bowl and allow to cool in the fridge for another 15 minutes.

Once chilled, mix with the chilled yogurt.

Nutrition:

Calories per serving: 233.

Carbs: 52.2g.

Protein: 3.5 g.

Fat: 2.9g

Deliciously

Preparation Time: 10 minutes

Cooking Time: 5 minutes

Servings: 2

Ingredients:

2 cups fresh lychees, pitted and sliced

2 tablespoons honey

Mint leaves for garnish

Directions:

Place the lychee slices and honey in a food processor.

Pulse until smooth.

Pour in a container and place inside the fridge for at least two hours.

Scoop the sorbet and serve with mint leaves.

Nutrition:

Calories per serving: 151.

Carbs: 38.9g.

Protein: 0.7g.

Fat: 0.4

Tostadas

Preparation Time: 15 minutes

Cooking Time: 15 minutes

Servings: 2

Ingredients:

½ white onion, diced

1 tomato, chopped

1 cucumber, chopped

1 tablespoon fresh cilantro, chopped

½ jalapeno pepper, chopped

1 tablespoon lime juice

6 corn tortillas

1 tablespoon canola oil

2 oz. Cheddar cheese, shredded

½ cup white beans, canned, drained

6 eggs

½ teaspoon butter

½ teaspoon Sea salt

Directions:

Make Pico de Galo: in the salad bowl combine diced white onion, tomato, cucumber, fresh cilantro, and jalapeno pepper.

Then add lime juice and a ½ tablespoon of canola oil. Mix up the mixture well. Pico de Galo is cooked.

After this, preheat the oven to 390F.

Line the tray with baking paper.

Arrange the corn tortillas on the baking paper and brush with remaining canola oil from both sides.

Bake the tortillas for 10 minutes or until they start to be crunchy.

Chill the cooked crunchy tortillas well.

Meanwhile, toss the butter in the skillet.

Crack the eggs in the melted butter and sprinkle them with sea salt.

Fry the eggs until the egg whites become white (cooked). Approximately for 3-5 minutes over the medium heat.

After this, mash the beans until you get puree texture.

Spread the bean puree on the corn tortillas.

Add fried eggs.

Then top the eggs with Pico de Galo and shredded Cheddar cheese.

Nutrition:

Calories 246,

Fat 11.1,

Fiber 4.7,

Carbs 24.5,

Protein 13.7

Mediterranean Baked Apples

Preparation Time: 10 minutes

Cooking Time: 25 minutes

Servings: 2

Ingredients:

1.5 pounds apples, peeled and sliced

Juice from ½ lemon

A dash of cinnamon

Directions:

Preheat the oven to 2500F.

Line a baking sheet with parchment paper then set aside.

In a medium bowl, apples with lemon juice and cinnamon

Place the apples on the parchment paper-lined baking sheet.

Bake for 25 minutes until crisp.

Nutrition:

Calories per serving: 90.

Carbs: 23.9g.

Protein: 0.5g.

Fat: 0.3g